The Basic Essentials of
CANOE POLING

by Harry Rock

Illustrations by
Michael Pusich

ICS BOOKS, Inc.
Merrillville, Indiana

THE BASIC ESSENTIALS OF CANOE POLING

DEDICATION

To my wife, Anne, without whose love and support my passion and success with canoe sport and poling would not be possible!

Published by:
ICS Books, Inc.
One Tower Plaza
107 E. 89th Avenue
Merrillville, IN 46410
800/541-7323

Library of Congress Cataloging-in-Publication Data

Rock, Harry
    Canoe poling : the basic essentials of / by Harry Rock.
        p.   cm. -- (Basic essentials series)
    Includes index.
    ISBN 0-934802-36-X : $4.95
    1. Canoes and canoeing   I. Title.

GV783.R63 1992
797.1'22--dc20   90-26423
                                                          CIP

TABLE OF CONTENTS

1. GETTING STARTED

While there are two distinct styles of canoe poling, this book will focus primarily on "power poling." This is the contemporary style which has developed out of the competitive poling ranks which has a strong freestyle flavor to it. It is sometimes referred to as "sport poling" by traditionalists. The primary difference is in the stance and what a poler can do using the squared off stance versus the diagonal stance. This predominant style is used today by most competitive and recreational polers. The advantage of the contemporary power poling stance is the ability to work both sides of the canoe for increased power and bow control when climbing pushy water and big drops. It also allows for increased maneuvering in rock gardens using slalom techniques.

While poling has long been associated as a utilitarian means of propelling a loaded canoe from one point to another, the development of modern techniques has brought many new converts over because of the ease of climbing upstream. Poling creates a sense of independence and self sufficiency by eliminating the need for shuttles. It opens up the ability to hit the waterways after work or when there is no one to boat with to help set up shuttles. The ability to push upriver and then paddle or pole downstream gives an individual a feeling of freedom in escaping the pressure and stress of everyday life and relaxing on the river. It temporarily removes the need for other people and creates an entirely isolated situation where you can become one with nature, taking in the peacefulness and tranquility of the land, water and animals. The sport can encompass itself from the challenges of running class III rapids to extending the boating season as the ultimate low water sport because of being able to pole through very shallow sections of water not navigable by paddle. As long as there is enough water to float on, its poleable. It is also an excellent form of river rescue because of the ability to push up through heavy water. The canoe can be held stationary in the middle of heavy current indefinitely by planting the pole on the bottom. The rescuer can either direct the rescue while in the main current, ferry stranded boaters to shore or use the pole as a reaching pole for pulling swimmers to shore. If nothing else, it is simply a great way to gain passage into small streams or explore rivers which have no upstream access. This can sometimes mean boating virgin water because paddlers are unable to reach remote upstream access points. Maine guides have long continued with the tradition of standing tall by using the big stick to move their clients into the backcountry and up the waterways to the pristine fishing and camping areas.

Equipment (poles, footwear, PFD, canoes)

The largest limiting factor in the development of canoe poling as a discipline has been the lack of adequate poles. There are very few commercial manufacturers and the ones who exist have difficulty in shipping single piece poles due to the length. Most sources have been from resourceful polers who have been able to acquire stock and manufacture end plugs in their basement and garage shops.

Pole Material

Fiberglass has been used but it has not proven durable, especially in the boulder strewn rivers of the northeast. The problem is the lack of lateral strength in the side walls once they are pinched between rocks. When the pole is inserted, it changes its vertical angle as the canoe moves forward which can jam it up against rocks. This creates pressure on the side walls and collapses them. The other disadvantage of fiberglass is its flexibility. As power is applied the pole bends tremendously. This creates a major control problem for the boater while trying to move upstream because the canoe will drift sideways, away from the desired path of travel until the pole begins to spring back.

The pole must be plugged with a synthetic material such as delrin or nylon to allow the pole to float if dropped and to absorb the wear and tear from the bottom. Its greatest advantage is that it does not pin between rocks like aluminum because of a low coefficient of friction. It does slip off rocks however when executing eddy turns.

Wood has long been the traditional material. River guides simply cut or find a suitable sapling of spruce or ash. The less adventurous of us can find stock at a local lumberyard and then shave it down. Some river outfitters carry commercially manufactured wood poles although these are not very common. The other alternative is to purchase a closet pole. It has a lot of flex, is weak and is not a good selection for long term use.

It is important to ensure that wooden shafts are splinter free. The end will also split apart if a steel shoe or brass sleeve is not fitted on the end to absorb impact and wear as the pole is planted on the rocky bottom.

The biggest disadvantage is the weight of wood. It is rather heavy and can become very tiring after extended use, especially after absorbing water. It also does not allow double ended use. The advantages are that the bottom plants are quiet compared to the clunking of aluminum and comfortable to hold during cold water use.

Aluminum has proven to be the top choice by most contemporary polers and racers. This has revolutionized the sport of big sticking because of its double ended capability. The light weight makes it very responsive for use from side to side and doesn't cause one to tire quickly. It is very strong and durable. It has flex, yet is stiff enough for total power delivery. It can be straightened if it bends as long as the wall isn't crimped which may cause it to break. Its disadvantages are that it is cold to hold in chilly water and it is noisy as it makes contact with the bottom. Aluminum must be plugged or it will sink. The choices are wooden dowels, cork, solid aluminum, or a solid synthetic such as delrin. Steel spikes are usually inserted into wood or delrin to assist with grip in ledge conditions and to reduce wear on the plug. Plugs must be flush with the outside wall to prevent pinning due to an extended lip. Aluminum is usually 6061 T6 aircraft tubing with diameter choices of 1", 1 1/8", or 1 1/4". The larger the diameter the stronger the pole and the less flex it has. Diameter size may be dictated by hand comfort and how much speed is desired in deep water conditions when using the kayak stroke for propulsion. The most prevalent choice among racers and recreational polers has been the 1 1/8 diameter with a wall thickness of .058"at a standard length of 12 feet.

Aluminum must be prepared before use because your grip will tend to slip on the smooth metal. This is accomplished by either roughening up the surface with a file, taping the pole with plastic tape (not duct tape), or by rubbing paraffin or bees wax over the entire length of the pole. This is similar to how surfers apply wax to their surfboards for traction.

Footwear

Proper footwear is critical to maintaining balance and delivering effective power plants. Tremendous thrust and leverage is generated during each power plant which must be transferred to the canoe through the feet. An aggressive rubber sole is required to prevent slippage. Feet should be cleaned before entering the boat to maintain a good surface to stand on. Dirt and sand can act as small roller bearings when force is being applied to the contact point between feet and hull.

Safety Items

A personal flotation device should always be worn regardless of the depth and difficulty of the water. The best choice is a type III over the shoulder vest because it offers floatation around the entire torso area. It provides protection against the elements and padding against rocks when taking those unplanned swims.

Helmets are recommended to protect the head in case of exits from the boat due to pole pins, missed pole plants and unexpected stops from impacting rocks. I have had pinned poles spring back sometimes as I tried to work them free making painful contact with my head.

Safety should never be compromised. Not only must you worry about your own welfare but also the well being of the rescuer who may have to come after you.

Canoe Selection

Part of the appeal of canoe poling is the ability to use any type of recreational craft, regardless of length, material or width. However the best overall boat for tracking ability and maneuverability is a standard recreational 16' ABS Royalex canoe. The longer the canoe, the better it tracks and generally the faster it is. The shorter the hull, the more maneuverable it is but the slower it will be and the tougher it is to track upstream. A full hull design at the ends is desired to reduce the porpoising effect from power plants along with a 15" center depth to shed waves. A 35-36" beam to enhance balance is also desireable. Canoes that immediately taper to the stern from the center thwart tend to sink in the stern when power is being delivered. ABS is preferred because of its ability to slide off rocks. Limited rocker is helpful for turning without causing a loss of tracking ability. A shallow "V" hull design helps with tracking and provides good initial and secondary stability because of having a "shoulder" to stand on versus a flat bottom hull.

Trim

Canoe trim is critical for successful upstream movement. The boat must be slightly stern heavy to lift the bow stem out of the approaching water. This keeps it from grabbing, tracking and pulling the craft off course into a wild uncontrolled ferry towards shore. The bow must be high enough to allow the current to slide under the hull. Driving the bow into current creates very difficult control problems.

Figure 1-1 Normal Trim requires the poler to stand 1-2 feet behind the center thwart causing a stern heavy trim so that the bow stem breaks out of the water to allow water to slide under it without tracking. Waterline length is now 1-2 shorter than the actual canoe.

As gradient steepens and as current increases, the more the bow must be lifted to clear. Climbing drops will sometimes dictate moving further back in the hull to create even higher lift to help break over the lip of the ledge.

Downstream travel requires flattening the canoe to increase wetted surface area for additional speed as long as the boat has reached or exceeded current velocity. The bow now parts water rather than pushing up waves like a powerboat at half speed. If the canoe is moving slower than the current, then trim must be adjusted so that the stern (upriver end) is higher than the bow (downstream end). This again is necessary to allow water to slide under the hull as the craft moves slowly downstream to keep it from tracking. The boater should be in front of the center thwart to create the bow heavy trim. The quickest and most secure way of changing body position in the canoe is by using small hops either forward or backwards. Trying to move each individual foot will cause the boat to rock sideways causing a possible upset. To change positions from one side of the thwart to the other you can either cross by walking the center line for stability or try a "Rock Hop" by jumping over the center thwart landing on the other side. Balance and care must be preserved to insure a secure landing. A great crowd pleaser!

Where polers stand in the canoe has a tremendous impact on the amount of speed and glide that is generated. Ideally, the canoe should be evenly trimmed with both ends drafting the same depth of water. The canoe can use its full length for maximum water displacement which allows it to float higher. It parts less water reducing resistance which results in higher speed and longer glide between power plants. Hull speed increases as waterline length increases. Therefore, if a 16 foot craft is weighted in the stern resulting in a waterline length of 14 feet, it will be slower than an identical craft which is properly trimmed. The higher the bow is, the more it resembles a power boat at slow speed pushing a large bow wave creating increased water resistance.

Because the dynamics of the power plant causes some down force on the hull, the rear half of the canoe must have a full shape before tapering to the stern to combat the sinking effect which reduces speed and glide. The bow tends to be pushed upward creating a wave for increased resistance. A fuller shape increases the wetted surface area displacement so that the canoe has more of a planing effect across the water rather than sinking and creating a stern rooster tail.

2. FORWARD PROPULSION

Stance

The "power poling stance" is the thing that has revolutionized poling and separated it from "classic style poling" which uses the diagonal stance. Almost all competitors incorporate the squared off delivery which allows the poler to work both sides of the canoe with ease. The poler should stand one to two feet behind the center thwart. This creates a stern heavy trim which helps with bow control when moving upstream. The feet should be spread as wide as possible, positioned under the shoulders and up against the chines of the canoe. Body position should be perpendicular to the midline. This wide stance provides tremendous control and balance as the boat pitches and rolls through the waves. Keep your knees slightly bent to act as shock absorbers with a slight forward lean of 10°-15° at the waist to enhance balance and leverage.

The biggest problem beginners have is developing balance. The following exercise is good for establishing balance and confidence:

1. Grip the pole like a kayak paddle and hold it waist high like a tightrope walker holding a balance bar.
2. Slowly start weighting and unweighting each leg by bending one knee and then the other to create a rocking motion in the canoe. All motion should come from the waist down; the upper body is practically stationary. This motion is very similar to the

weighting and unweighting used in downhill skiing.
3. Speed up the rocking motion until each gunwale touches the water, emphasizing control.
4. Then try just weighting one leg and holding the gunwale as close to the water as possible without taking in water. This helps build balance and boat control.

Practice this exercise each time you get out on the water so the canoe begins to feel like an extension of your body. Remember that your feet should never move relative to the bottom of the canoe during this exercise. In time you should be able to weight one side of the canoe and lift the unweighted foot completely off the hull while standing stationary on the other foot. With practice and balance, this will usually be a good crowd pleaser!

Power Delivery

To generate forward propulsion, one must understand the mechanics of the power plant which is the primary source of straight line movement in a canoe using a pole. Like paddling, unless proper technique is applied, canoe speed and direction will be misdirected and slow.

Study and concentration of proper execution and technique will result in an efficient use of energy transforming into top speed and distance traveled. Boaters need to be selfish in conserving energy while achieving maximum results. This helps accomplish established goals whether it is winning races or just enjoying a cruise on a river. This lesson is pointed out only too well from watching world class athletes who make things look so easy with little apparent effort. Their technique is very stylish showing a high degree of finesse. It is this finesse that makes them the best in their discipline, achieving maximum results with minimum output. They exude efficiency by minimizing energy expenditures.

Power Plant Techniques

The power poling style of poling has revolutionized the sport. This style is most commonly equated with what racers use in competition. Canoe legend Bill Mason, after watching me with fascination at a canoe symposium, compared it to free style paddling by taking a traditional discipline and developing a new aspect with no restraints. What was once thought of as just a "grunt and grind" means of pushing upriver is now fun, challenging and exciting. We actually look forward to going out for a "big push with the stick." The transformation of this esoteric form of canoeing into something that has gained national recognition as a

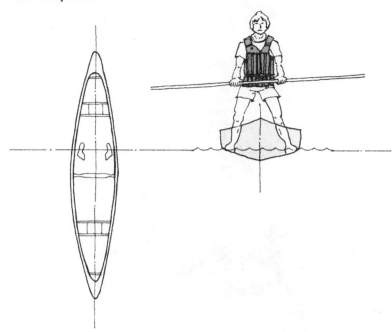

Figure 2-1 Power Poling Stance spreads the poler's feet against the canoe chine for balance, perpendicular to the canoe's midline and 1-2 feet behind the center thwart to create a stern heavy trim.

Figure 2-2 Power Poling Body Position requires wide foot placement for balance, perpendicular to the canoe's centerline. Note the slight knee bend, forward lean of the upper body, high hand placement and forward pole angle for powerful leverage off the bottom.

Figure 2-3 Balance is critical for successful poling without taking unexpected swims. Start by slowly rocking the canoe from side to side using the legs as pistons weighting and unweighting while keeping the upper body motionless. Finally try standing on one edge while picking the opposite foot up off the bottom for developing maximum balance.

respected discipline has to do with the stance. By squaring off the traditional diagonal stance into the power poling stance of today, an entirely new arena has opened up for river maneuvers and skills to use the pole to accomplish these. To understand power poling, one must study its makeup including pole angle, leverage, and power delivery.

Pole angle. This component has a major impact on the effectiveness of power poling. For forward movement, the pole must always by placed behind the boater, resulting in a forward angle of the pole. Ideally the angle should be about 45 degrees. Too often beginners plant the pole in front of their body and try to pull the canoe past the pole. This position creates very poor leverage because the plant has no weight on it to keep it in place. The pole is also in a vertical position which tends to create all upward force rather than forward force on the canoe. The body is pulled forward and off balance because there is no way to stabilize it against the pulling motion.

Leverage. With proper pole angle, effective leverage can be applied. Because the desired result is forward motion, the ideal situation would be

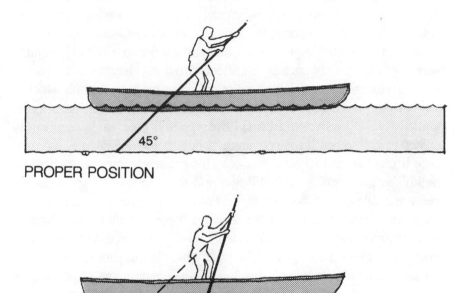

PROPER POSITION

OBTUSE ANGLE: PUSHES STERN DOWN

ACUTE ANGLE: POLE KICKS OUT

Figure 2-4 Power Pole Position should be at 45°for combined bottom purchase and forward force. If the pole is at an obtuse angle it causes the stern to sink due to down force with limited generated forward force. If the pole is at an acute angle the pole will tend to slip and kick out due to the tremendous force being applied.

a wall placed behind the canoe after each glide phase so that the pole could be planted against it in a horizontal position. This would create total forward force on the canoe for 100% efficiency. Unfortunately, this is not possible so a compromise of a 45 degree angle is made by planting on the bottom. As a result, two forces are created as power is applied on the pole. In a weightless environment, theoretically the canoe would jettison into the air at a 45 degree angle to the water surface because of the generated force. Because gravity negates this affect, two things happen to the canoe. First, the stern tends to sink because of the down force on the hull which is why a fuller hull design is important. Second, as the canoe reacts to the applied force, it moves forward. Leverage and pole angle are closely aligned to each other. If the pole angle is greater than 45 degrees more up force is created than forward motion. This creates a porpoising effect on the hull as the stern is pushed down and then pops back up when the pressure is released. If the pole angle is under 45 degrees, less down force is created on the hull and more forward force is generated, which is desirable. However, the pole plant tends to slip out because there is less down force to hold it in place. The pole which is buoyant wants to float upward. Sometimes when passing large boulders, you can plant the pole against the dry portion of the rock to gain pure straight line power.

Power Delivery. Once the pole has been planted with proper angle, you are ready to deliver power. Both hands should be placed as high as possible on the pole with thumbs on top in a batters grip to maximize range of motion. The hands will usually be spread apart by several inches or whatever feels comfortable. The offside hand should be on top of the onside (pole side) hand. As force is applied, the large back muscles should be used to pull the hands past the hip before releasing pressure. As the hands approach the hip, the upper torso should begin a slight rotation in the direction of the pole to ensure large muscle involvement and to aid full range of motion of the hands passing the hips. Once the leverage motion begins, proper pole angle is necessary to maintain bottom purchase and keep the plant from slipping. After acceleration is underway, the force on the pole diminishes somewhat reducing the amount of down force required to hold it in place. Now the poler can concentrate on forward force production. As a result, he/she can begin sinking with the body and bending at the knees while maintaining the same upper body angle. This can be compared to leaning against the wall with your legs in a sitting position without a chair. The forward leverage on the pole keeps the body from falling backwards. The sinking motion helps to reduce the pole angle relative to the water surface to generate more forward force and less up/down force on the canoe. Sinking of the body also helps maintain balance. The more forward force that is generated, the more the body must lean back against the pole to keep from being pushed over frontwards.

Hand Over Hand Technique

This technique is very effective for climbing steep drops, moving against strong current and for people who don't have strong upper bodies. Simply plant the pole behind you at a 45 degree angle and start climbing the pole by placing each hand over the other and pulling forward until you reach the end of the pole. Bend your knees and lean away from the bow to help push the canoe forward and to preserve balance. (This hand motion is like the one kids use on a bat when picking sides for a softball game.) For additional power, finish off the motion with a power plant when you reach the end of the pole.

Figure 2-5 Hand Over Hand Poling is an effective means of climbing upstream without a great deal of effort. Commonly known as "climbing the pole" it simply requires moving your hands up the pole placing one hand over the other until reaching the end.

Pole Recovery

Pole recovery is very important when traveling upstream. The longer the pole is off the bottom, the more momentum you'll lose, particularly when you're climbing drops and fighting accelerating water being funnelled into a chute. Minimum recovery time is of the essence for maximum power delivery and constant headway against the current. All three of the following recoveries can be used with either power plants or hand over hand techniques.

Pool Cue. This is the fastest and most efficient method for pole recovery when climbing upstream. At the end of either a power plant or a hand over hand plant, form a circle around the pole with the thumb and forefinger of your onside hand, similar to the one used by pool players. Then quickly thrust the pole upward with your offside hand which starts out on top of your onside hand to send the pole sliding forward and up through the pool cue hand which remains next to your hip. The end of the pole should exit the water and pass just inches over it to reduce drag through the water. Once the pole is fully extended, bring both hands together as high as possible and let gravity return the pole to the bottom by releasing your grip and allowing the pole to drop.

Figure 2-6 Pool Cue Recovery is the fastest of the recoveries and most effective for climbing steep pitches. The lower hand encircles the pole like a pool cue using the thumb and forefinger, while the upper hand gives a rapid upward thrust of the pole so that it regains its original position by sliding through the lower hand.

This should be a very fluid motion which requires practice to master. The pole will fall nearly vertical but the forward motion of the canoe will return it to a 45 degree angle before you load it again. In particularly fast flow, you actually may have to force the pole down into position to keeps the current trying to sweep the pole downstream.

Windmill Recovery. This technique is very effective on flat water or easy upstream and downstream sections. After power is applied, the pole is simply flipped end-over-end so that the wet end becomes the dry end and vice versa after each power plant. This generates more power plants per minute than any other recovery, resulting in greater speed. The pole always remains on one side of the canoe with this recovery. The disadvantage is that the pole reenters the water vertically when you're moving downstream and it tends to pin or jam between rocks. As a result, you may need to let it go (down the creek without a pole) or risk bending the pole or being catapulted out of the back of the canoe. When moving upstream you can't gain effective leverage off the bottom because there is no forward angle on the pole once it is planted. This is caused by resistance on the hull which limits forward glide because of the opposing current. Because the canoe does not glide past the pole once it is planted you are left with a forward pole angle of 25 or 30 degrees rather than the optimal 45 degrees.

Figure 2-7 Windmill Recovery is usually used in shallow flats or easy upstream and downstream sections of water. The poler keeps the pole on the same side of the canoe, rotates it 180 degrees and uses the opposite end after each power plant. The lower hand reverses its grip. Reaches down and flips the pole over for replanting. The other hand remains stationary, and provides a point of rotation for the pole.

This is the easiest recovery for beginners to learn. The biggest problem newcomers have is keeping the canoe moving in a straight line. Follow these steps:

1. After you've completed the power plant, release the onside hand and turn it over with palm up.
2. Reach down and regrip the lower half of the pole so that the thumb is facing the water.
3. Rotate the wet end up and over (counter clockwise) with the onside hand while using the offside hand as the point of rotation and to direct the dry end towards the water, thus changing contact ends. The point of rotation should be hip or waist height.
4. Release the offside hand just as the pole enters the water and regrip on top of the onside hand (both thumbs are on top in the batters grip).
5. Lift your hands high to reposition for the next plant and loosen your grip so the pole slides through your hands. Begin the next power plant once the pole has regained bottom purchase.

Crossover Windmill. This is the same motion as the windmill except the pole alternates sides of the canoe. This is very effective for climbing a stiff current and maintaining bow control. The motion of crossing over the hull easily sets the pole up with an immediate 45-degree angle in the water ready to provide effective leverage.

The difference between this and the windmill recovery is that the offside hand guides the dry end of the pole down and across the hull into position on the other side. The onside hand continues bringing the wet end up and into position. The previous offside hand now becomes the onside hand and regrips the pole below the other hand. Let's break it down step by step. Note that the onside and offside positions will reverse with each cross-over move.

1. After you've completed the power plant, release the onside hand and turn it over with palm up.
2. Reach down and regrip the lower half of the pole so that the thumb is facing the water.
3. Rotate the wet end up and over (counter clockwise) with the onside hand while using the offside hand as the point of rotation to direct the dry end towards the water on the opposite side of the canoe. The point of rotation should be in

front of the body at mid waist. The offside hand should guide the pole from one side of the body to the other as the pole is making its rotation so that it now becomes the onside hand.

4. Release the new onside hand just as the pole enters the water and regrip below the new offside hand (both thumbs are on top).

5. Lift your hands high to reposition for the next plant and let the pole slide through your hands. Begin the next power plant once the pole has regained bottom purchase.

6. The pole should be parallel to the midline of the canoe once it is planted so that pure forward force is generated after the pole is loaded with power.

Rudder Action

Whether you're paddling or poling, the canoe can be a very pesky craft. It doesn't want to move in a straight line and it will try to take the scenic route among the bushes and rocks near the shore. Learning to

Figure 2-8 Cross Over Windwill is a windmill recovery that alternates sides to combine speed of recovery with improved bow control in stiff current. The top hand provides the point of rotation for the pole, while the lower hand reaches down with a reverse grip to flip the pole 180 degrees and direct it across the boat.

generate pure forward force will help eliminate the unpredicted turns but you'll also need to learn how to rudder.

Ruddering is a sure way of maintaining a straight course, especially when pushing along on flat water or mild upstream stretches. Most beginners will find this helpful for maintaining directional control until power strokes are mastered, providing pure forward force. At the end of every power plant, simply allow the pole to float up and drift behind the canoe for two or three seconds. This is usually enough time to have an affect on the bow. If more correction is required, simply move the pole in or out with your lower hand (onside) and the bow will quickly respond in the direction the pole was moved to, either left or right. Then execute the desired pole recovery for the next power plant.

As your technique improves, you'll need to rudder less and less. While you're learning, however, keep these points in mind:

1. The slower the boat is moving, the more the bow will tend to wander, so some forward speed is necessary to keep yourself in a straight line.

2. Too much correction is often worse than not enough. Many novices, upon seeing the bow swing off by five or 10 degrees, will counter with 20 or 30 degrees of correction. Remember, you only need to correct enough to bring it back where it started. It's much like baking a cake; just because the recipe calls for a pinch of salt doesn't mean you put in a cup full to make sure you have enough. Just add the right amount to end up with the desired result.

Controlling Your Bow

The success of all canoeists, whether paddler or poler, has been the ability to control the bow of their canoe and make it go where they want it to, not where the river decides to take it. The mark of the accomplished boater is the ability to control the bow and move the canoe where they choose to. Nowhere is this more noticeable than poling upstream. The key to successful upstream travel is keeping the bow pointed directly into the oncoming water. As soon as the bow falls off a degree or two the canoe will begin to ferry and move away from the desired path of travel. Unless a quick correction is made the angle of error will rapidly grow in magnitude. There are several factors to keep this from happening.

Trim

Trim of the boat is a critical item. The canoe must have a stern (downstream end) heavy trim. This keeps the bow (upstream end) stem of the craft from grabbing and tracking off course. The approaching water is able to flow under the bow without issue and you can effectively determine direction. Hull leans, leg drive and pole leverage are all factors in helping to move the bow around easily as long as the bottom can slide easily without resistance from the bow.

Power Delivery

The way power is applied to the canoe will determine how well upstream direction is maintained. You must remember that when power is generated on one side of the hull, the boat will automatically veer to the opposite side. Perfectly executed power plants will minimize this but it is a natural factor to deal with. The best compensation other than corrective strokes which slow the canoe down is to simply alternate sides using cross over windmill recoveries so power is being delivered evenly. This will automatically correct angle error.

Reading Water

Knowing how to read water and use it to your advantage is a very important skill to master. Recognizing where the current is coming from will determine how straight a course you will travel. Looking at the shore line can be very misleading because current sometimes moves diagonally. You can assess water direction by watching for bubbles, leaves, sticks and eddy lines. These are all excellent indicators as to where water is moving. The bow must be pointed directly into the approaching water so there is equal resistance on each side of the hull, causing the boat to move in a straight line.

Pole Plants and Recovery

The choice of power delivery will make a difference in how easily you ascend waterways. Essentially there are two options based on position in the river. If you are climbing up the middle of the channel, then power is going to be required on each side of the hull for automatic course correction using the cross over windmill recovery for alternating side power plants.

If you are hugging the shore line, then a pool cue recovery, which keeps the power delivery on one side, is appropriate. Pole plants should be restricted between the boat and the shore. This enables the poler to keep the bow in towards the shore and out of the main flow by pushing the stern out if the bow starts to drift out. It is much easier to move the stern in or out than the bow which has constant frontal resistance on it because of the downstream flow.

Power plants or hand over hand plants are appropriate based on current strength and incline gradient. Power plants are more powerful but they are tiring. Hand over hand plants are slower but easier to execute, especially in steep climbs. An important factor to keep in mind at all times is that the slower the hull speed, the harder it is to keep the bow in line and the more it wants to drift. Recovery time between plants must be kept to a minimum to maximize the number of plants per minute. As soon as the power phase ends and the recovery begins, hull speed drops immediately. If it falls to less than that of the current, the boat will stall and begin to drift backwards at an angle making correction and recovery very difficult.

Deep Water Technique

People always question how I traverse deep water because of their assumption that I must be confined to shallow water with a 12 foot pole. My answer is that water depth doesn't make any difference. They are always amazed to see how fast I am able to move through deep water. Whether you are pushing along the lake shore or shallow river sections, sooner or later you have to cross deep water to reach the opposite lake shore or to cross pools separating rapids. Contrary to what most people think, movement of a canoe with a 1 1/4" diameter pole using a modified kayak stroke is quite fast. An efficient solo poler can easily maintain the same pace as a team of paddlers. This appears impossible to most observers due to the lack of paddle blades on the pole, but the key is the amount of leverage the poler is exerting on the water and the number of strokes per minute being executed. Easy cruising with an improved vantage point makes this an interesting alternative to sitting and paddling for many recreational boaters. I generally start classes out using the kayak stroke because of beginners ability to pick it up immediately, thus they experience instant success and are turned on to the sport. It is also an easy way to help beginners develop balance.

At first most people will start out stiff legged, upright and just using arms during pole rotation. However, correct technique is needed to make for the most efficient and energy conserving style possible. The following will break down the technique into two components, upper and lower body motion.

Figure 2-9 Kayak Stroke is used for traversing deep water. It incorporates upper torso rotation with a near vertical pole for efficient forward pull along the gunwale. At the same time the legs are weighting and unweighting like pistons to create a slight rocking of the canoe in coordination with the upper body motion for surprising speed and efficiency.

Upper Body

Upper body motion should by very smooth and rhythmical. The pole should enter the water with little splash and limited noise culminating in an even pull and clean exit. Follow these steps for proper technique:

1. Stand in the power poling stance and grip the pole shoulder width or slightly wider, equal distance from the middle. Your thumbs should be facing each other.

2. Lean forward 15-20 degrees, with your knees slightly bent to increase balance and leverage.

3. Rotate your onside shoulder forward, as you would in a kayak, so that the onside arm can reach well ahead to plant the stroke near the gunwale at the front of the canoe.

4. Insert the pole two to three feet into the water with the pole as vertical as possible, eliminating any side sweeping action. There should be a slight bend to the onside elbow with the offside arm being bent and almost horizontal at the catch position (the point at which the pole has entered the water but before power is applied).
5. Begin to rotate or uncoil the torso at the waist to that the large back muscles are doing the major work, not the smaller arm muscles.
6. Continue the power phase past the hip and then recover into the next by rotating the lower hand up for a clean exit.

The stroke should pull evenly and in a straight line, parallel to the desired direction of travel and very close to the side of the canoe to prevent any loss of forward power. As the stroke ends, the upper body is immediately prepared for the next stroke (on the other side of the boat) because the shoulder plane has already rotated forward. The pole should make a ripping noise as it moves through the water without any splash.

Lower body

Your legs should constantly move using a weighting and unweighting motion similar to the bicycling motion you would see in marathon paddling. As the pole pulls back and the upper hand moves across the frontal plane the body, the offside leg unweights and bends slightly at the knee. The onside leg is weighted and pushes down. A rhythmic action results matching up with the upper body motion. This causes the boat to rock slightly from side to side allowing for an extended reach and pole extension into the water during the forward rotation of the upper body. The increased extension is because the onside rail is lower to the water and out of the way of the pole. The leg motion is not very exaggerated.

Practice on flat water is highly recommended to develop technique and rhythm before entering moving water or rapids. You should be able to move in a straight line without taking multiple strokes on one side at a time. Course correction can be made by simply stroking a bit further from the canoe using a modified or regular sweep stroke.

3. TURNING

Sweep Strokes

All of us who stand tall with a big stick need to have the ability to change direction quickly or to make angle corrections at some point in our travels. Proper technique and effective leverage accomplish these tasks with a minimum of strokes and energy.

The pole can be used to gain leverage for hull alignment from the water or off the bottom, whether running down a wave train of standing waves, climbing upstream through complex rock gardens or just spinning to turn while in flatwater.

Sweeps are probably the most important strokes used in poling since draws and pries are not possible. They are very effective for eddy turns and peel-outs because they provide forward power as well as turning force.

The sweep stroke, whether with paddle or pole, is one of the most poorly executed strokes by boaters. What should be a 180 degree range of motion often turns into 140 degrees or less. Boaters are often sloppy in starting the stroke about 20-30 degrees away from the bow and ending it just as far away from the stern. They don't take advantage of the greatest point of turning torque in the stroke but preserve the forward force, which often sends the boater speeding ahead into trouble without turning. Remember that the first and last 45 degrees of a full

23

sweep provide the greatest leverage for turning. The middle 90 degrees are mostly forward propulsion. Let's discuss the different aspects of sweeps.

Hand Position and Motion

1. Place your hands on the pole at shoulder width or a little wider if comfortable. Position is similar to holding a kayak paddle. The pole should be held waist high.
2. Grip the pole as you would a kayak paddle, both thumbs on the inside, shoulder width apart.
3. Extend the pole full length to one side so that the offside hand is gripping the end of the pole (If extending the pole to the right, the left hand grips the end). The onside hand is over the water while the offside hand is waist high in front of your midsection.
4. Extend the pole in a near horizontal position with one to two feet of the far end in the water as far ahead of the bow as possible.
5. Sweep the pole around in a full arc of 180 degrees keeping the opposite end as far away from the pivot point of the canoe as is feasible. The further the pole's leverage end is from the canoe, the greater the turning torque. Both arms and hands will extend over the water (outside the canoe) at some point in the arc to further increase the leverage.
6. Torso rotation should occur during all sweeps to take advantage of strong back muscles and their greater torquing power. A wider range of pole motion also results from the rotation.

Range of Motion in the Forward Sweep

In analyzing the sweep angle, let's assume the bow is 0 degrees and the stern is 180 degrees. The bow is also 360 in a complete circle.

1. 0 to 45 degrees: The pole starts swinging away from the hull in a lateral (sideways) motion and pushes the bow in the opposite direction. (see Figure 3-1b)
2. 45 to 135 degrees: Rather than a turning force, this portion of the sweeping arc creates more forward motion on the canoe and is very helpful in maintaining momentum while changing

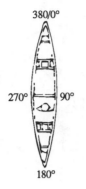

380/0°   a

270°   90°

180°

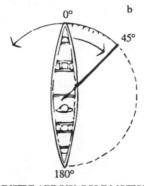

0°

45°

180°

• INSIDE ARROW: POLE MOTION
• OUTSIDE ARROW: HULL MOTION

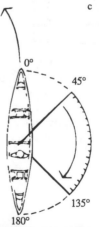

c

0°

45°

135°

180°

• INSIDE ARROW: POLE MOTION
• BOW ARROW: HULL MOTION

Figure 3-1 a,b,c Range of motion.
  a: four basic angles
  b: 0° — 45°

c: 45° — 135°

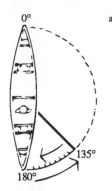

a

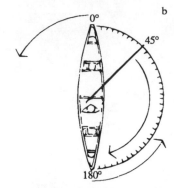

b

• INSIDE ARROW: POLE MOTION
• OUTSIDE ARROW: HULL MOTION

• INSIDE ARROW: POLE MOTION
• OUTSIDE ARROW: HULL MOTION

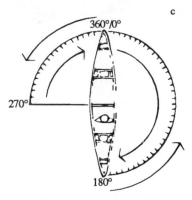

c

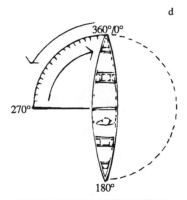

d

• INSIDE ARROW: POLE MOTION
• OUTSIDE ARROW: HULL MOTION

• INSIDE ARROW: POLE MOTION
• OUTSIDE ARROW: HULL MOTION

Figure 3-2 a,b,c,d, Range of motion.
a: 135° — 180°   b: 0° — 180°
c: 270° — 180°   d: 270° — 360°

direction. It also prevents the canoe from being pushed downstream by the current when turning upstream. (see Figure 3-1c)

3. 135 to 180 degrees: The pole sweeps toward the stern. This action pulls the stern laterally toward the pole and swings the stern under the bow. As the most powerful part of the sweep, this phase generates the greatest amount of turning force on the canoe. (see Figure 3-2a)

4. 0 to 180 degrees: By incorporating the above listed portions you start by moving the bow sideways away from the pole, produce forward power and then pull the stern sideways towards the pole completing the spin. (see Figure 3-2b)

5. 270 to 360/0 to 180 degrees: This powerful application is accomplished by reaching over the bow using a cross draw motion and pulling the pole through the water toward the bow (the motion resembles the dynamics of an eddy turn). The stroke draws the bow toward the pole. Upon reaching the bow, the poler quickly lifts the pole over the boat and reenters the water next to the boat to complete the remaining 180 degree sweep. (see Figure 3-2c)

On the cross draw, you can reach as far as 270 degrees for extra power, but you need good flexibility and balance. The twisting action and ensuing leverage can create some uncomfortable stress on the upper torso, knees and ankles. There's also the potential for loss of balance and an unexpected swim if the excessive twisting force on the lower body causes your feet to slip. (see Figure 3-2d)

Boaters must generate just enough force to accomplish the desired move. Sweeping the last 45 degrees (from 135 to 180) is sometimes enough to make a quick angle correction. In other situations a force of 90 to 180 degrees is required for forward momentum as well as turning. For radical turns needing an immediate spin, a full 180 degrees or even 270 degrees is necessary

When polers get into trouble, the cause is usually from a sloppy sweep (an arc of 45 to 165 degrees). They become frustrated by the boat's reluctance to turn and fail to realize that they are not negotiating a full range of motion. Polers lose the most powerful portion of the sweep stroke and continue with additional incomplete strokes. You end up driving the boat straight into a rock or the bank because more forward power is delivered than turning force.

In all cases unweighting the offside of the boat when spinning enhances the turn. The lean creates rocker and reduces frontal resistance against the boat's leading edge as it spins.

Reverse Sweeps

Reverse sweeps (180 to 0 degrees) are very useful for negotiating a quick turn in the opposite direction. Hand motion and grip remain the same. The sweep starts from the stern and moves toward the bow . I find it awkward to continue the sweep past 90 degrees because of weak and inefficient leverage from pushing forward on the pole rather than pulling. I also don't recommend reverse sweeps when you're running upriver because it slows the canoe too much due to the reverse thrust being created on the hull, thus pushing it backwards downstream.

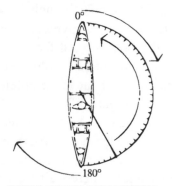

• INSIDE ARROW: POLE MOTION
• OUTSIDE ARROW: HULL MOTION

Figure 3-3 180° — 0°

A greater range of motion is possible by over-rotating the body and beginning the reverse sweep from the 200 degree mark before sweeping the pole toward the bow. The length of the pole (and the extra height from standing up in the boat) will allow you to pass the pole over the stern and continue the sweep toward the bow without lifting the pole from the water.

To create a more explosive reverse sweep, I lay the pole's grip end (approximately two to three feet from the end) on my onside hip which is used as a fulcrum. I then push my hip out as I pull the pole in with my offside hand which creates much greater leverage on the water. My hands grip the pole on each side of my hip to initiate the action.

A 360 degree motion can be accomplished with a combination of moves. Let's try one on the left side of the canoe. Begin with a reverse sweep (180 to 270 degrees), and then quickly shift your hands into a cross-draw position when the pole is perpendicular to the canoe's midline. Release your right hand from the pole while swinging your left hand with the pole up past your head and behind your body into the cross draw position (the same pole end remains in the water throughout this move).

Your right hand regrips the pole just below the left hand with your palm facing downward. The left hand releases the pole and regrips the end with the palm facing downward and with thumbs on the inside facing each other. The sweep continues (270 to 360/0 degrees) to the bow, over the bow and then into a forward sweep on the other side (0 to 180 degrees). This move creates a very powerful and fast spinning action on the canoe.

Bottom Plant Turns

In shallow water you can plant your pole off the bottom for leverage to produce powerful turns and spins. This is much more effective than trying to use sweeps as there is no slippage of the pole in the water. The pole is set firmly into the bottom and then pulled against in a forward sweeping motion to create hull spin. As long as the pole does not slip, the boat will spin quickly. Lets go through the steps to make this happen correctly.

1. Plant the pole four to six feet off the side of the canoe and forward of the center thwart. The upper grip hand rests at eye level. The pole will be at an approximate angle of 45-60 degrees. Hand position should be using the kayak grip so thumbs are on the inside, shoulder width apart.
2. Unweight the opposite gunwale to create rocker and to eliminate frontal resistance on the offside as the canoe spins in that direction (the boat edge nearest the pole plant is weighted).
3. Apply leverage to spin the boat. The offside hand (on the high end) pushes the pole while the lower hand pulls to create force.
4. Use the knees and thighs to drive the bow around by transferring the force generated from the pole to the boat

itself. You should push the weighted knee and foot (nearest the pole plant) forward to help drive the bow around. This motion is similar to a skier who weights the right ski in a snowplow turn, and then turns to the left as a result.

5.   As the stern nears the pole, release the leverage and replant the pole forward of the center thwart to continue the turn.

Another application is to use a planted cross draw. Start by crossing over the bow with the pole to plant it on the bottom in a cross draw position. The pole is near vertical. Pull the bow toward the pole and then release leverage upon reaching the hull. Lift the pole over the bow again to replant as previously described. Use caution because the cross draw motion creates a twisting torque on the lower body which can cause your feet to slip. Don't forget to use upper torso rotation to create stronger force and a wider range of motion.

With these techniques and a little practice you should be able to change direction quickly and effectively.

U-Turns On The River

A major accomplishment (and source of anxiety) for every beginning whitewater canoeist is avoiding those rocks which suddenly appear out of nowhere. As skills and confidence develop, those same rocks become exciting challenges behind which you try U-turns.

Eddy turns and peel outs are not only fun but are necessary skills to any accomplished boater. The ability to leave the main flow and seek protection behind an obstruction (an eddy turn) is crucial. The ability to re-enter the main current without capsizing (a peel out) is equally important. It affects proper negotiating of complex rock gardens, the ability to assist with rescue operations, avoiding potentially dangerous routes and the ability to take a breather when things are not going well.

Effective moves have two components, an understanding of water dynamics and a physical ability to spin the canoe. A symbiotic relationship exists between the two components. One is unable to function effectively without the other. Let's explore the dynamics of each and how to blend them together.

Eddy Currents

An eddy is created by anything that obstructs the path of moving water such as boulders, ledges and inconsistencies in the riverbank. Bends in a river cause eddies on the inside of the turn. As water hits an obstruction and is displaced around it, a void is created behind the obstacle. As the hollow attempts to fill itself, the water swirls into it

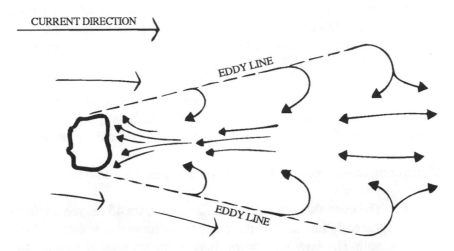

Figure 3-4 Eddies are created by anything that obstructs the path of moving water. A void is created behind the obstacle which the river attempts to fill in by sending water swirling in from the downstream side of the rock creating an upstream current. An eddy line separates the opposing main flow current and the eddy current to create a current differential.

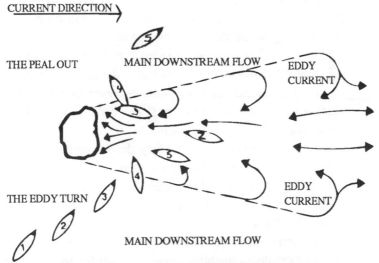

Figure 3-5 U-Turns are necessary skills for effective, safe and fun river running. For eddy turns build up momentum at position 2 and begin the turn at position 3. For eddy turns, use a cross draw motion to place the pole against the upstream side of the rock to apply leverage to help execute the turn at position 4. For peel outs, plant the pole downstream on the eddy line, unweight the upstream gunwale to allow the bow to swing downstream in position 4. Don't forget to always lean downstream of the entering current whether it is the eddy or main flow for either type of U-Turn.

from downstream and creates an upstream current. The two opposing currents, the main downstream flow and the upstream eddy current, create a current differential which is separated by a line called the eddy line. A canoe that properly crosses this line spins due to the opposing forces acting upon the hull.

Eddy Turns

Eddy turns are to canoeing what linked turns are to skiing. The canoeist ability to control the river is similar to how a skier controls steep terrain. Each person uses turns to control speed and for traversing desired routes of descent.

These components prepare the canoe for entry into the eddy:

1. The canoe should enter at an approximate 45 degree angle to the eddy line so that the current differential can work on the hull. The bow will be pushed upstream once it crosses the eddyline while the stern continues to swing downstream, until the entire canoe rests in the eddy water and is parallel to the upstream eddy current.

2. The bow should enter as close as possible to the head of the eddy to take advantage of the strongest point of the current differential. This positioning initiates the spin by holding the bow in place while the stern swings around.

3. Canoe speed has to be controlled when entering the eddy or the boat may overshoot it and leave the eddy before the spin begins. Momentum is important however because the main current can sweep the boat past the eddy if it lacks enough forward speed to enter the eddy.

4. The size and power of the eddy determines the speed and angle of entry. The stronger the eddy, the sharper the angle and the higher the speed that can be used for successful entry. If an eddy is small or weak, the canoe must be almost perpendicular to the eddy line with limited forward speed to ensure entry. Be careful with particularly strong eddies as they can create an unstable base of water for the canoe to rest in because of the upswirling currents from the river bottom.

Now let's look at the use of the pole in helping to execute the eddy turn.

CURRENT

EDDY LINE

Figure 3-6 Eddy Turns are used to enter an eddy from the main current at a 45 degree angle as close to the rock as possible. The poler extends the pole in a cross draw position and applies leverage on the upstream side of the rock.

1. As the canoe approaches the top of the eddy with the proper angle of entry, you should quickly extend the pole to the downstream side of the canoe. Grip the end of the pole with your offside hand. Both hands should be shoulder width apart using the kayak grip.

2. Just as the hull starts to cross the eddy line, lift the pole over the bow in a cross draw position. Then apply leverage with the far end of the pole on the upstream side of the boulder. This leverage helps to force the bow behind the rock. A word of caution is very important here. As the leverage is applied against the rock, quite a bit of twisting torque is put on the body which may cause your feet to slip and cause you to fall or even exit the boat.

3. As the canoe begins to swing, you should start unweighting the onside leg (downstream side) to cause the boat to lean into the turn (like a bicycle leaning into a sharp corner). This

unweighting keeps the onside edge from grabbing water, being sucked under and capsizing the boat. The lean also changes the hull configuration in the water by lifting the ends, creating more rocker and allowing easier spinning.

4. Sometimes a sweep stroke can be used before entering the eddy to help initiate the turn. With particularly powerful eddies, sweep strokes alone will drive the bow into the eddy while the main current swings the stern around. Make sure you have angled the boat properly with enough lean.

Peel Outs

Many of the same principles apply to peeling out of an eddy. Angles, leans and eddy line placement are the same.

1. Establish a 45 degree angle to the eddy line in preparation for exiting just behind the rock.
2. Use one power plant to drive the boat halfway across the eddy line to take advantage of the current differential. The pole should be on the downstream side of the canoe for the power plant.
3. Now quickly reposition the pole downstream of the boat about six feet away. The end should be planted on the eddy

Figure 3-7 Peel Outs are used to enter the main stream from an eddy at a 45 degree angle to take advantage of the resulting current differential. The poler exits halfway out of the eddy, plants the pole downstream on the eddy line and then leans on it for balance while unweighting the upstream gunwale. This created rocker allowing the hull to spin faster.

line or just inside the eddy. You should be using the batters grip with both thumbs on top. The onside hand should be extended straight down the pole with a slight break in the elbow while the offside hand is placed at chin or eye level.

4. Lean on the pole for balance and unweight the offside gunwale (upstream side) to expose the boat's bottom. The downstream current will jet the bow around while the opposing eddy current pushes the stern upstream. Exit near the top of the eddy but far enough away from the obstruction so the stern has room to swing around without hitting it.

5. The canoe will now enter the main flow while pivoting around the planted pole. The hull must spin into the main current or the boat will stall on the eddy line or remain in the upstream eddy current. Complete the peel out by converting the pole plant into a forward power plant for reaching river speed to help you pick your line of travel.

6. When peeling out of powerful eddies, cross draw strokes and/or sweep strokes are often enough to pivot the boat once the eddy line is crossed after step two. Care must be taken to compensate for the tendency of the downstream flow, when in contact with the upstream side of the hull, to try to suck it under and cause a capsize. Boat lean is very important to avoid this.

Using Leans to Turn

It is fascinating to watch a young racer go against an older experienced racer. It is usually a contest of strength and power versus technique and finesse. The seasoned competitor uses years of experience to help shave seconds off his/her time. This translates into an understanding of moving water and how to make the canoe respond effectively. It has often been said by many racers who are well into their career that they wish they knew then what they know now! Where these racers once relied on power to perform moves, they now save time and energy with an educated approach. They read water conditions and use the shape of their boat to react quickly. They are able to minimize mistakes and recover quickly from the ones they do make. An important part of their "education" is a knowledge of the design shape and how it affects the boat's response. There are several factors which allow this to happen which we will explore.

Design Factors

Rocker is the amount of banana shape which is built into the bottom of the canoe. The more the ends turn up, the shorter the waterline and the less frontal resistance that is created on the side of the canoe as it spins. Rocker can be created by weighting one side of the canoe. Because of the curved design of the side as it is tilted, the ends will naturally lift out of the water. This reduces the wetted surface area, shortens the waterline which allows a quicker spin.

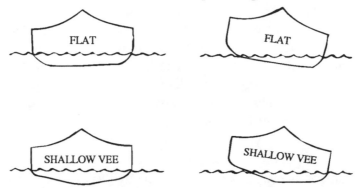

Figure 3-8 Profile Characteristics of the hull determines the level of stability when leaning the boat for a turn. While the sharp chine will allow both to carve a turn, the shallow V shape provides a shoulder to stand on for greater final stability and for additional leaning ability without fear of upsetting.

Chine/edge. Webster defines chine as "the juncture of the bottom and either of the sides of a boat." The amount of chine a canoe has determines how effectively it can be used. The sharper the chine, the more it can be edged into the water to carve a turn. This is done by weighting the offside chine (right side if it is a left turn) so that it catches the oncoming water which forces the craft around. Canoes with bottoms that are flat, V-shape, or modified Vs are most effective because of their pronounced edge. Round bottoms have a diminutive edge so they are not able to slice into the water as well. Decked boaters have long used this technique because of the pronounced edge on their boats.

Hull shape. The center thwart pushes out the canoe sides and creates a natural curvature. As the canoe travels through water it encounters equal frontal resistance on each side of the bow. If the canoe is tilted to one side, its shape in the water is like that of a protractor with a straight edge on one side and a curve on the other.

Because the resistance is only on the side of the curvature, the hull naturally turns in the direction of the curve. Marathon racers commonly use offside leans to minimize correction strokes and to change direction. The fuller the shape of the hull, the quicker the canoe responds. Marathon and Olympic canoes are very sleek with almost a straight line from the bow to the widest point and back to the stern. As a result they are less responsive than a recreational canoe with its greater flare beginning at the bow.

Manual Application

Now lets take our knowledge of design factors to actual maneuvers. Our ultimate goal is to become one with our craft to achieve

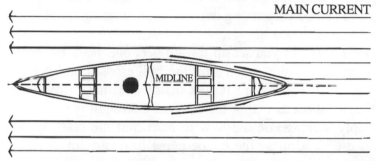

Figure 3-9 shows that an evenly weighted canoe will move in a straight line due to equal frontal resistance on each side.

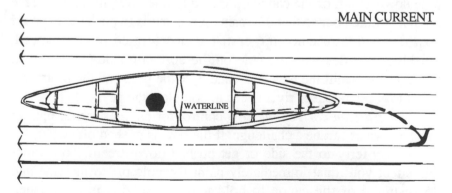

Figure 3-10 shows that by weighting the left side releases the frontal resistance on the right side so that the canoe naturally turns to the right. This is also promoted by the hull's natural curvature. (Note that the dotted line is the new waterline do to being weighted to one side.)

efficiency and top performance. Let's look at how to integrate these moves. Note that the eddy turn and peel out section in this chapter involves a different application than what is described earlier in this chapter.

Eddy turns. Approach the eddy as described previously. As you cross the eddy line from the main current, instead of using a cross draw, plant the pole on the downstream side of the canoe within the eddy and four or five feet from the boat. For effective leverage, grasp the pole's upper half about three feet apart using the kayak grip so that the thumbs are facing each other. Weight the onside edge (closest to the pole) so that it catches and carves around. At the same time apply leverage on the pole to help force the bow around. CAUTION: Centrifugal force on the canoe can be very strong depending on entering speed causing the canoe to upset.

Peel outs. As you set up for the peel out, plant the pole on the upstream side of the canoe after the hull crosses half way into the main current. Placement is just inside the main flow with hand position identical to that in the eddy turn. Weight the upstream edge and apply leverage on the bow to help spin the craft downstream. Again use caution as the canoe can flip upstream as the current catches the weighted edge and tries to suck it under. This maneuver is best used in lighter water conditions.

In heavy water, make a traditional eddy turn by placing the pole downstream of the canoe on the eddy line. Weight the pole side (onside) of the boat so that the main current starts to push the exposed bow downstream. Once the craft has accelerated to river speed, quickly shift sides with the pole on the upstream side (as described earlier) and weight the new "on" side. Use the pole and the protractor effect to accelerate past river speed to complete the peel out.

Upstream correction. Bow control for polers pushing upriver in heavy water can be a challenge. If the bow is pushed off center, the canoe may ferry to the side or get pushed downstream. To counter this effect you must immediately plant the pole off to the side and downstream of the canoe to hold it in place so it is not pushed backwards. Once your position is stabilized you should weight the downstream edge. The canoe will immediately begin to point back up into the main current. Applying leverage on the pole at the same time also helps push the bow back into position.

Straight line correction. The canoe will tend to veer off course at times when you are attempting to propel it in a straight line. Rather than take time to apply corrective action you can simply weight the edge opposite the desired direction of travel so that the protractor effect will then allow the canoe to carve around. For example, weight the right side if the canoe drifts to the right. This action releases any resistance on the left side so that the natural curvature and the frontal resistance on the right side force the canoe to the left.

As anything, this all takes practice to master. However, once mastered, it will add a new dimension to your boating control and technical ability. You will find eddy moves and upstream travel much easier as you begin to let the design of the canoe work for you.

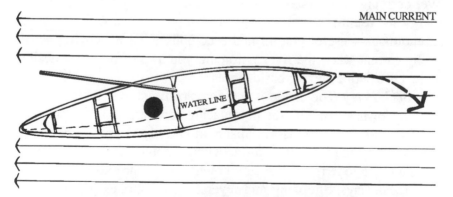

Figure 3-11 When veering off course while moving upstream in heavy current, set the pole on the downstream side to hold the canoe stationary and then weight the downstream edge to release the frontal resistance on the exposed side. The natural curvature and released water pressure will cause the hull to quickly swing back into position for continued upstream movement. (Note that the dotted line is the new waterline due to being weighted to one side.

4. FERRYING

Lateral Moves

Ferries are a critical skill for canoe polers to master whether their objective is racing or just plain fun. Crossing a river by ferrying is a common maneuver and an important part of a poler's repertoire of skills.

Effective ferrying is necessary when scouting rapids, running a river or trying to shave seconds while racing. It lets you tap the river's energy and use it to supplement your own power. You will experience an enormous sense of control and accomplishment in moving across strong current when the river is forcing you away from your desired route. Let's define the two basic ferries:

Back Ferry. The canoe is moving slowly (slower than the main current) downstream with the poler facing downstream in the standard position with the stern as the upstream end of the craft. The canoe should be angled so that the upstream end is pointed towards the shore you are trying to ferry to. The current will contact the exposed side and push it sideways. Snubbing and reverse kayak strokes will slow the boat's descent. The heavier upstream end will tend to swing in the current and make the canoe difficult to control because of moving slower than the current. You can minimize this effect by stepping over the center thwart and standing in front of it. This action changes the

40

trim and weights the downstream end. Be careful when changing ends of the boat as it can potentially cause an upset.

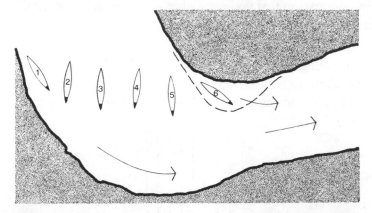

Figure 4-1 Back Ferries are used to traverse a channel while facing downstream using snubs or kayak back strokes to slow the downstream progression of the canoe. The upstream end should be angled in the direction of travel.

Forward ferry. You are facing upstream in the standard position with the bow as the upstream end of the craft. Forward power plants will counter the downstream force of the current. The lighter upstream end offers less resistance and makes this ferry easier to control. The bow should be pointed in the direction you wish to move towards so that the water will strike the exposed side and push it sideways.

If executed correctly, ferries are simply a use of boat angles and current direction to provide lateral motion. The boat moves perpendicular to the current or diagonally downstream depending upon the river's speed.

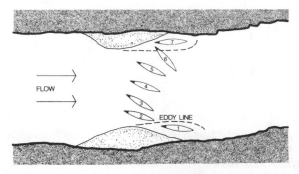

Figure 4-2 Forward Ferries are used to cross channels while facing upstream using power plants to prevent downstream drift. The bow is angled in the direction of travel to create lateral push. The boat must exit the eddy quickly to avoid being spun downstream due to the current differential.

Three variables affect the success of ferries: boat angle, amount of generated power against the current and pole plants. Let's assume in the following discussion that you are facing upstream and current direction is 0 degrees.

Boat Angle

Establishing proper boat angle is the less experienced poler's biggest problem. Lateral movement is created by exposing one side of the canoe to the current. Current strikes the upstream side and pushes the canoe to that side.

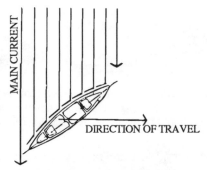

Figure 4-3   Boat Angle During The Ferry is critical to ferry across a river. By exposing one side of the canoe to the main current, the water strikes the upstream side of the canoe pushing it laterally across the channel.

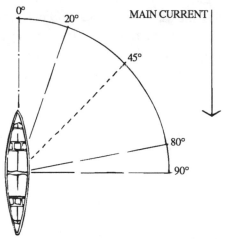

Figure 4-4   Selecting Boat Angle is an important skill for effective ferries. Ferry angles are usually between 20 to 80 degrees depending on current speed and desired routes. Polers often maintain a 45 degree angle. Angles of 0 to 5 degrees result in boat stall and loss of position in the river. Angles of 80 degrees or greater result in the canoe slipping downstream sideways.

Too little boat angle (0 to 5 degrees) fails to expose the canoe to the current and stalls it.

Too much angle (80 degrees or greater) exposes most of the canoe and blows it downstream broadside.

Keep the following factors in mind:

1. Point the canoe's upstream end toward the chosen destination across the river.
2. Know the direction of the main flow in determining proper boat angles.
3. Be aware that current direction often changes as you cross the river and you may have to adjust your angle.
4. Proper boat angle is between 20 and 80 degrees depending on the speed and power of the current. You will work with a 45 degree angle most often.
5. The stronger the current, the less angle necessary for the lateral push.
6. Tighter angles (20 to 30 degrees) are easier to control and can be opened if necessary. Wide angles are very difficult to close up in heavy water and may subject you to moving downstream sideways, a very dangerous and possibly costly move to your canoe.
7. The wider the angle (30 to 80 degrees), the greater the hull exposure and the stronger the current's lateral push. Wider angles result in faster lateral movement.
9. Spills often occur when leaving the eddy because the boat is subjected to an opposing current trying to suck the upstream edge under, thus flipping the canoe over.
10. Use proper boat lean to minimize upsets (always lean downstream).

Leaving eddies deserves some caution. A good strategy is to begin with a small angle to get a feel for the current and then widen the angle if necessary. Leave the eddy quickly with good power and get the boat fully into the main flow. If the boat straddles the eddy line too long, the main current can grab the upstream end and spin the boat around sending you downstream and possibly causing a spill.

Boat lean is crucial! It should change as the canoe moves from the main current into the eddy because of the different directions of the two currents. The boat's upstream edge must be unweighted at all times to prevent the current from sucking it under and upsetting the boat.

Pole Plants

You will usually find that the safest and most effective way to plant your pole once the ferry is underway is on the upstream side of the canoe (the side opposite the direction of travel). This strategy prevents the boat from moving into a planted pole upsetting the canoe or bending the pole after you run it over. If planting on the downstream side, extend the pole to its full length and plant it as far as possible from the canoe and keep in mind that the current will try to push the canoe into the pole.

Remember these basic principles:

1. Plant the pole close to the canoe and two to three feet behind yourself on the upstream side of the canoe.
2. Apply power in a diagonal direction to push the canoe both laterally and forward. The canoe should be moving away from the pole.
3. Expend limited energy during the power phase. Power plants should only generate enough power to counter the downstream force of the main current and to push the canoe across the channel smoothly.

Improper boat angle will send the canoe off course. The bow will usually swing downstream and you are then faced with a difficult correction back to the proper angle. Extend your pole on the downstream side and use 180 degree sweeps for correction. The combination of forward power and corrective action drives the bow upstream and pulls the stern back under the bow.

Concentrate on the last 90 degrees of the sweep where you will be most effective in changing the boat angle. The canoe's upstream end usually has the strongest resistance against it because the main current strikes it first, causing considerable frontal resistance. It resists efforts to be pushed upstream. The downstream end encounters less resistance because it is moving with the main flow and can be pulled much easier below the bow.

Forward Power

Forward power is an integral part of effective ferrying. You will find that you have to change the amount of power required to follow your chosen route. The degree of power you use determines whether the boat moves perpendicular to the current or diagonally upstream or downstream.

Remember these basic principles:

1. Forward power must be equal to current speed to move perpendicular to the current.
2. To move upstream, forward power must be greater than the current speed.
3. To move downstream, forward power must be less than the current speed.

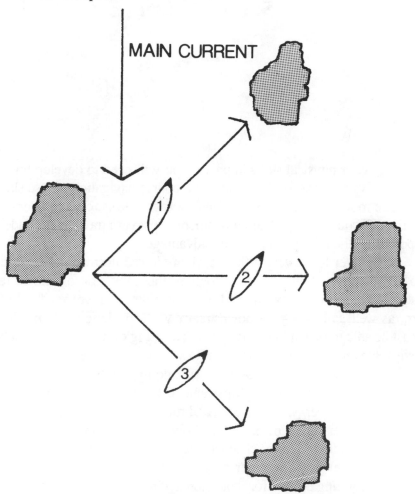

MAIN CURRENT

Figure 4-5 Route Strategies still determine the amount of angle and generated power.
1. Climbing upstream requires greater forward power and a tighter angle.
2. Perpendicular movement requires power equal to the current speed and more angle.
3. Slipping downstream requires less forward power that the current speed and a wider angle.

5. DIRECTION

As your physical skills improve, you will need to develop highly refined river reading skills for effective course navigation. These skills must be more exact than those of the average downstream paddler due to the difficulties of upstream movement. Upstream travel is dependent upon using the river power to one's advantage.

The river looks very different when viewed upstream as opposed to downstream. You have to recognize the back side of eddies for picking out the weak trailing end of eddy water, and where eddy lines are, as well as looking for downstream Vs from the closed end. You must be able to pick a line to run upstream using every eddy possible to gain some protection from the main flow.

Try to take advantage of every situation possible to make it work to your benefit for moving upstream efficiently with a minimum expenditure of energy. Here are several rules to keep in mind:

1. Water runs slower and shallower near the shore than in the middle of a river channel. This is due to friction between the water and the river bottom. Stay along the shore when running upriver for protection against the main flow.
2. Water wants to move in as straight a line as possible. The only reason it changes direction is because the river bed dictates it by meandering. Water will move to the outside of a

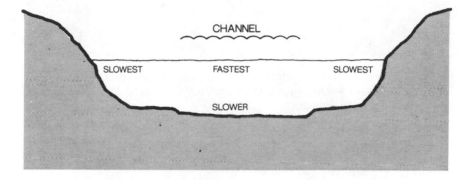

Figure 5-1 Straight River course selection has the poler staying to the outside edge for the slowest water when moving upstream. Downstream travel utilizes the middle of the channel for the greatest water.

bend because it is trying to go straight and is forced to turn when it encounters the bank. The majority of the water is going to be on the outside of the bend making it the deepest part of the channel and the fastest, most powerful water. For protection against the main flow and ease of travel, stay to the inside of a river bend to find shallow water and to catch upstream eddy currents when available. Eddies always exist on the inside of a river bend because the river is trying to fill in a void created from the main flow bypassing it as it runs to the outside of the bend.

3. Because water moves in a straight line unless pushed in another direction, erosion always occurs on the outside of a bend. Beware of roots, downed trees causing strainers and

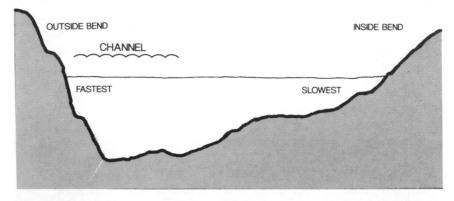

Figure 5-2 River Bend course selection requires the poler staying on the inside bend for the slowest water when moving upstream and staying to the outside when heading downstream for the fastest water.

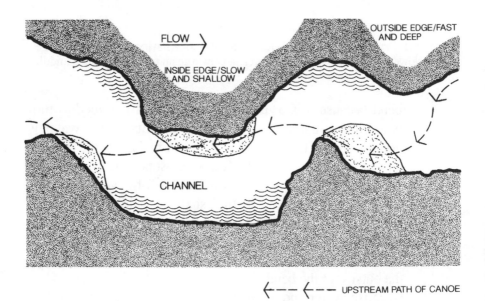

Figure 5-3 Upstream Travel requires the poler to work all the inside bends of the river to catch upstream eddy currents and to avoid the powerful downstream flow.

trapped debris. Also be alert to the fact that the water is going to try to push and pin you against the outside shore where the greatest force of water is.

4. When running upstream, line up behind rocks in heavy water (no matter how far away) to gain protection from the main current. Trailing eddy water can extend quite a way downstream depending on the size and strength of the eddy, so use it to your advantage and try to get a little upstream help from the eddy current.

5. Try to pick a route that allows leapfrogging and eddy hopping from rock to rock for constant protection from the current. This may involve ferries to make the move from rock to rock but it will also conserve energy when moving upstream.

6. In shallow water conditions, use the opposite reasoning for picking a line. Because the conditions are going to be bony, you will need every extra inch of water possible which will make the difference between floating or scraping through. Run to the outside of the bend where the deepest water is. Because of the low conditions and lack of water, there will be less force trying to push you against the outside bank.

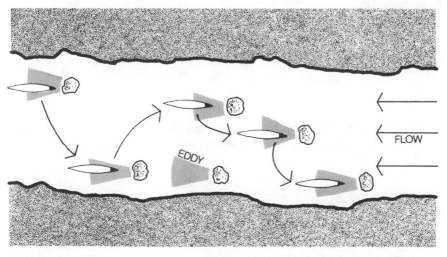

Figure 5-4 Eddy Hopping from rock to rock when traveling upstream in stiff current is crucial to gain protection from the main flow and to catch upstream eddy currents.

7. Recognize that water is going to follow the fall line which is the path that a ball would take if you were to let it roll down a decline. As a result water won't always move to the outside of a bend if there isn't enough power to force it there. It may move to the inside if the fall line draws it there because of how the river bottom is cut.

8. When running downstream, take the exact opposite course as you do when moving upstream. You now want to take advantage of every amount of downstream power possible for maximum speed and energy conservation. Avoid crossing eddies which will slow you down because of the upstream current and stay to the outside of the bend for the fastest, deepest water.

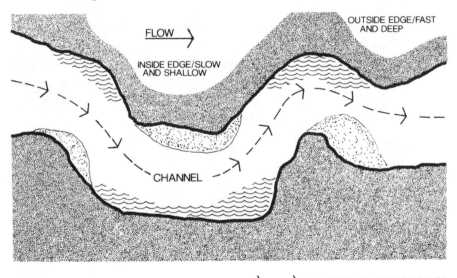

Figure 5-5 Downstream Travel requires the poler to avoid all eddies created by the main channel and to remain in the downstream flow for maximum speed and to access river power.

Sideslipping

Sideslipping is an important skill for negotiating river position whether you are traveling upstream, downstream, or preparing to exit an eddy. You need to have the ability to move your double ender sideways to improve your angle and position for negotiating a particular section of river without losing either the canoe's parallel alignment to the current or being pushed backwards when moving upstream. In paddling, you learn to use combinations of draws and pries to slide the canoe. Because draws are impossible with a pole, you have to use the closest thing to a pry, a lateral power plant. This skill comes in very handy when preparing to exit an eddy. You may have to move the canoe sideways across the eddy to set up the peel out without changing the necessary angle for crossing the eddy line. Sideslipping is a bit different depending on which direction you are heading in current so lets explore the factors involved with both.

Figure 5-6 Sideslipping is used to change lateral position in the river for improving upstream course direction or to suddenly avoid downstream rocks when descending. The poler unweights the offside leg to decrease the frontal resistance on the leading edge of the canoe and then pushes sideways with short, aggressive power plants.

Upstream. When climbing upstream, you always have the current trying to push you back downstream. Sideslipping is typically used to adjust your angle prior to climbing a drop or for sliding into an eddy's wash to gain some protection from the main flow. When facing upstream you have to contend with trying to move laterally as well as maintaining your present position. The key is to plant the pole downstream of you to counteract the force of the current. The pole should be in close to the canoe to prepare for the power application and on the side of the canoe opposite the direction you wish to move towards. Hand position will be two to three feet apart with the offside (top) hand being just below your jaw next to the onside shoulder. Use a batters grip with both thumbs on top. As you start to apply power, unweight the offside of the canoe to drop the onside (pole side) gunwale close to the water. This action reduces the wetted surface area, breaks the bow stem out of the water shortening the water line, and allows water to slide off the bottom as the boat moves sideways away from the pole. It also prevents the leading edge of the canoe from grabbing and rolling underwater (from increased frontal resistance on the canoe as it moves laterally). Use short power plants to move the boat laterally. The plants should be in a diagonal direction to provide force both in the direction of travel and forward power to counteract the downstream push on the canoe. Use leg drive and pressure with your feet to help maintain the canoe's parallel position to the current. Make sure that the pole exits the water cleanly after each plant to minimize drag on the water. I find that a modified pool cue recovery is best for repositioning the pole for the next plant.

Downstream. Downstream movement requires quick reflexes and the ability to move the canoe sideways as you travel because the faster you move, the quicker those pesky rocks seem to jump out at you. Sideslipping is a bit different now because you are continuing to move forward with the current. It is more difficult to execute because the canoe is moving past the point of pole purchase with the bottom. You have to plant the pole forward of the canoe so that it will provide some braking as well as lateral push as the canoe moves past it. There isn't as much lateral action on the hull as when the canoe is stationary because the forward motion is absorbing some of the lateral motion. The unweighting action probably won't be as accentuated because of the forward direction requiring more balance and stability than when moving the canoe from a stationary position. There should not be drastic side movement as it usually requires only inches of movement to clear a rock. It is important to keep forward speed under control to help negotiate complex routes. The faster you move, the faster things start to happen and the less time you have to compensate with correction.

Stationary water. Calm water is the easiest to sideslip in, be it flat stretches of river or behind eddies. It is simply a matter of planting the pole next to the canoe so it is parallel to the center thwart. Weight the onside gunwale and push away from the pole keeping it at right angles to the midline of the canoe. Hand grip and position on the pole should be the same as described above. Small power plants with pool cue recovery should be applied. An exaggerated, unweighted motion is possible to help reduce the wetted surface area and surface friction, thus increasing the lateral movement after each power plant. Subtle pressure on the pole either forward or backward while applying power will help correct the canoe's angle if it starts to drift at all. It is very important to master stationary water sideslipping before applying it in moving water, so practice, practice, practice!

Upstream Travel-Tips and Methods

Upstream travel against heavy current and rapids is what separates canoe polers from paddlers and what provides that special feeling of accomplishment and victory against the ever relentless downstream current. There is a tremendous sense of satisfaction in knowing that you are truly among a select few who can move effectively, efficiently and rapidly upstream. There are a few talented paddlers who can make their way up some surprisingly difficult water but they are nowhere as fast or efficient. Most paddlers end up either lining up, wading in waist deep water, pushing and/or pulling their boat, or portaging up to quieter water upstream. The upstream ability of poling creates true independence for boaters by eliminating the need for shuttles and providing a sense of self sufficiency. For me it is the primary attraction of the discipline. Essentially we take the best the river has to offer and we beat it at its own game by using that raw power to our advantage to help us move in harmony with the river.

The sense of satisfaction that rock climbers feel after conquering a difficult rock face or the way backpackers feel upon reaching a mountain summit is how canoe polers feel after beating upstream against waves, heavy flow, and a constant effort by the river to push the canoe downstream. I derive a natural euphoria from this very physical experience where I mentally, physically, and emotionally meet the river on its own terms, defy normal standards of travel direction and reach the top of a rapid. This is all accomplished through a simple understanding of angles, leverage, river reading ability, and a willingness to be patient and work hard. Let's review how these different elements all play a part in effective upstream movement.

Bow Control

The most essential component to moving upstream is total control of your bow. It is a combination of the factors we just read about. Bow control is clearly the factor that separates top racers from the rest of the pack and what creates more frustration among boaters trying to move upstream than anything else. There are three key elements to consider.

1. *Trim.* Establishing proper canoe trim is the most important factor in successful bow control. You need to have a stern heavy trim so the bow breaks out of the water and does not track. Driving the bow into current creates very difficult control problems because as soon as you are just a few degrees off center, the canoe will begin to veer off course and head for shore at a rapid pace. Its angle will usually increase making it more difficult for correction. You should be standing approximately 1.5 to 2 feet behind the center thwart. Be aware of the tendency to creep forward and begin to brace against the center thwart as it will only weight the bow and drive it into the current. As the water difficulty increases, it may be necessary to move further back in the canoe to pick the bow up higher to clear the rough conditions.

2. *Current alignment.* You must always have a sense of where the water is coming from, regardless of the river bank configuration. The canoe midline should always be parallel to the current direction so equal water force is striking each side of the hull. Should the force become disproportionate in any way, the canoe will immediately veer off course at a speed proportionate to the current's power. Constant observation of bubbles, leaves, sticks, eddy lines and river gradient is essential for proper assessment of water direction. You will find that the current always has small changes as you move along which will require minute amounts of correction because of eddy wash, river bed inconsistencies, channel movement and obstacles such as downed trees, boulders, flood debris and pinned canoes.

3. *Pole plant alternatives.* Your bow control can be improved by hugging the shore and using a hand-over-hand power plant technique while executing all your pole plants between the boat and the shore. This strategy will keep the bow tucked into the shore to prevent the current from pulling it back into

the main flush. If the bow starts to drift out, simple use the pole to push the stern out which will force the bow back in. I find that the most effective means of power is by using short but powerful power plants to provide constant forward motion so that forward speed does not stall. Otherwise the bow will start to slide out into the current. The hand-over-hand technique with pool cue recoveries help produce constant forward power with less effort than using power plants, especially when climbing steep pitches. In particularly difficult water I strictly use short power plants on the shore side of the canoe with rapid and forceful pool cue recoveries which don't break the surface (to reduce recovery time between plants) to keep the canoe from being pushed backwards.

As you become more adventuresome and powerful, moving right up the middle will be an inviting challenge. The cross-over windmill recovery is necessary to maintain the constant bow correction demanded by stiff current. By alternating sides, you ensure forward movement and bow control. Power is generated and course direction is automatically corrected on each side of the canoe. This is a physically demanding approach. Pole plants must always be behind you to gain leverage off the river bottom. If you allow the canoe to drift back after planting the pole, the pole will end up vertical in front of you. As a result, you lose all your leverage and the boat will continue to drift downstream. A sudden lack of balance because of overextending forward may also cause an unpremeditated wet exit from the canoe!

Exiting Eddies Upstream

Part of effective upriver work is the use of eddy hopping. This practice of seeking protection from the main flow by using the upstream eddy current behind a boulder is an important component of making the river work to your benefit. The only drawback is that it does position you behind boulders which may be very difficult to break away from if there is a powerful current creating strong eddy action. Eddy wash can create a very strong suction which will keep the canoe in the eddy and pinned against the rock. You must ensure a swift reentry into the main current so that the current differential has little opportunity to force the canoe drastically off course by spinning it because of the opposing forces being exerted on each end of the canoe.

The best strategy is using power plants on the eddy side of the canoe so that the pole plant is between the canoe and the rock as it is passed. This move ensures a breakaway from the rock and its eddy suction as well as providing strong forward movement of the canoe upstream. Pole plants on the river side of the exiting canoe will only serve to pin the canoe against the rock, thus stopping forward progress and leaving the boat in unstable eddy wash, thus putting it in danger of taking on water breaking over the top of the rock.

Climbing Drops

As you move upriver, you will eventually come up against the same drops that paddlers love to run down through. Poling up over a drop is what makes the sport so challenging and exciting. To me it is the most energizing move you can make on the river. Many people are intimidated by drops but they are not difficult if negotiated properly.

You first need to line up in the eddy at the bottom of the drop about two feet behind the ledge. Your canoe should be on the inside edge of the eddy line with just enough angle to break out of the eddy so that the canoe will be parallel with the main flow as it reenters. Once your reentry angle is ready, use a very aggressive power plant to drive the bow into the middle of the tongue of the chute. If there is enough forward momentum the bow will pop up on top of the tongue. A second rapid power plant or hand-over-hand plant will send the rest of the canoe up and over the drop to the next higher level. It is critical that the canoe's forward speed not stall or you will be pushed down backwards. Most drops are lined with boulders on each side of the tongue so use these to your benefit. It is perfectly acceptable to brace one side of your bow against one to help guide the canoe as you move up the chute. Because the current picks up a great deal of velocity as it drops over the ledge, bow control can become much more difficult. As you improve your control you should be able to climb drops without the aid of side boulders and move right up the middle of the chute.

Pinned poles are very common when climbing drops because of the amount of forward leverage you are placing on it. Poles have a tendency to jam between whatever cracks or crevices they come in contact with. As a result, you will come to a sudden stop which will feel like your arm is being torn out its socket or, as I have observed, the poler being pulled right out of the canoe. Nevertheless, your forward momentum will stop, making it very difficult to continue forward without being driven back again. It is possible to push up from a dead stop while half way into the tongue, but it requires a very strong power plant to overcome the current.

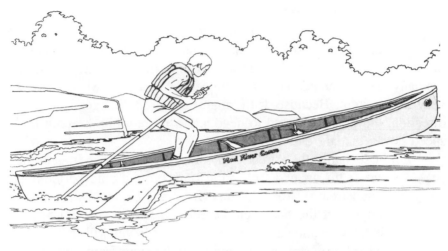

Figure 5-7 Climbing Drops is what poling is about, separating polers from paddlers. Use an aggressive power plant to send the bow out of the eddy into the middle of a downstream tongue of water. This action forces the bow to pop up on the top of the tongue. A second power plant propels the canoe up and over the top to the next ledge.

Drops up to three feet in elevation can be climbed easily. Taller drops are difficult because of the waterfall shape. Most of them start to pour water into the craft before it has a chance to pop up. Generally what happens is that the bow is driven right into the tongue at right angles. Standing further back in the canoe will help bring the bow up higher to help break through but you may have to look for another drop that is cut with flatter angle so that the bow will have a chance to enter and pop up. The shape of the hull can also have a major impact on how well it climbs drops, as a fuller bow will tend to ride up and over much better than a narrow, sharp bow which will pencil in without riding up as quickly, thus taking in more water.

Downstream Travel-Snubbing And Wildwater

As you start downstream after a long, hard climb, it is reminiscent of the reward that a rock climber experiences when rappelling after a tough climb or the sensation the crosscountry skier feels while skiing down after reaching a mountain peak. The biggest problem you will encounter will be controlling your speed for proper river reading and controlled navigation. The faster you move, the quicker things start to happen, the faster rocks suddenly appear in front of you, and the less times you have to correctly react to it. Here are two techniques you can use for effective downriver travel.

Snubbing

This classic downstream technique uses short poling jabs (snubs) off the bottom to control speed and course direction. Snubbing is typically used when descending technical rock gardens where there is very fast current. Because of the many required changes in course direction, the poler is forced to negotiate a route while keeping hull speed slower than the current.

1. First change the trim of your canoe by standing in front of the center thwart and facing the bow (you should be looking downstream). Your distance from the center thwart is the same as if the boat were heading upstream, about 1.5 to 2 feet. By creating a bow heavy trim, the water will slide under the stern (upstream end) and keep the stem from tracking as the canoe slowly moves downstream.

Figure 5-8 Snubbing is used to negotiate technical boulder strewn sections where a slow descent is necessary to select the correct course. The poler stands in front of the thwart to create a bow heavy trim so the stern does not track in the faster downstream current.

2. You should be in the power poling stance for maximum stability. You can also control the boat angle by using leg drive and pushing forward with one leg and then the other to help swing the upstream end around maintaining hull alignment. Maintaining a parallel relationship to the current is critical for boat control.

3. Extend your pole directly in front of you to prepare for the first snub. Your onside hand should be holding the top end of the pole and it should be at eye level. The offside hand will be placed about two feet lower down on the pole depending on comfort and effective leverage. Both hands should be in the batters grip with thumbs on top.

4. The pole angle is the same as when poling upstream, about 45 degrees depending upon forward speed and desired braking. A flatter angle creates greater leverage off the bottom and increased braking power. The pole should be directly downstream of the canoe with a parallel alignment to the midline of the boat.

5. As you move downstream use short forceful snubs to control and slow your descent. Be aware of the pole's tendancy to jam between rocks because the added pressure from the force of the canoe moving with the current. As the canoe approaches the pole, the pole angle will naturally increase as it moves more and more towards a vertical angle because of you moving closer to it. This will usually cause it to pin or jam between rocks because its exit angle is different from its entry angle. To counteract this you must use very quick and short snubs so that the pole is exiting at close to the same angle it entered. When executed properly you can achieve surprisingly tight control down very technical sections with no clear channels.

Wildwater

This downriver technique is used to run courses at speeds equal to or greater than the river current. It works best in channels requiring limited course direction. You stand directly behind the center thwart to create a more streamlined waterline by dropping the bow down, and you use power plants or kayak strokes for accelerated forward speed. Note that your pole will have a tendency to pin on the bottom when using power plants because of the radically changing exit angle due to the speed downstream. Little problem exists with tracking by the stern. In picking a course, you follow the main flow and avoid crossing any eddy lines because the upstream eddy current will slow forward progress.

Quick changes in course direction are necessary when rocks suddenly appear. The most effective technique is sideslipping to one side or the other as described earlier in this chapter. Remember to unweight the offside to break any downward suction of the leading edge as the canoe moves laterally sideways. Then use short and forceful power plants perpendicular to the canoe to push it sideways. These power plants may have to occur quickly at times with many changes of direction from side to side depending on how fast rocks suddenly pop up in front of you.

When running through a river bend, take into consideration the lateral drift that occurs because of the water trying to drift in a straight direction to the outside. You need to compensate for it by entering the bend on the inside third of the channel just outside the eddy line. As you move through the bend you will drift closer and closer to the outside shore so that if your alignment is right, you will exit the bend on the outside third of the channel in the fastest water but not so close as to worry about being pinned against the outermost bank.

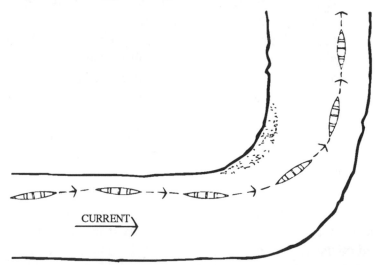

Figure 5-9   Large River Bends, when heading downstream in fast water, require positioning on the inside of the bend to compensate for lateral drift by the current. The canoe moves through the turn to avoid being pinned against the outside shore.

Leg action is very important in downriver running because you are usually encountering waves, holes and pillows (rocks just under the surface not always noticeable until you are right on top of them). You have to have the balance and ability to weight and unweight as you hit these disturbances to keep from taking in water and to allow the bow to pass over rocks just under the surface. By unweighting as you come up against a large nondirectional wave, you increase the height of the wave side of the canoe so that it is a higher obstacle for the wave to break over, thus taking in little if any water. When encountering rocks before having time to move laterally, simply unweight the side of the canoe to create a reduced wetted surface area and narrowed water line width. The canoe will now pass right over the rock without impact or without creating any drag. This technique also allows you to pass through channels that are smaller than your normal water line width by the canoe passing through on its side rather than full bottom.

The one caution of wildwater is the quick build up of downriver speed. You have little time to analyze the river conditions and react to them properly. The most effective means of reducing speed and regaining control if necessary is to back paddle using a reverse kayak stroke. Remember that the slower you travel, the more control you will have.

Reverse Moves

An important skill to have whether poling or paddling is the ability to run down channels in reverse or to perform maneuvers backwards. There are times when you'll get spun around after hitting a rock or if you don't make a ferry and you have to run down backwards because there isn't time or room to pivot. The highest percentage of unexpected spills is when the canoe is perpendicular to the main current. Instead of only requiring channels the width of the canoe, you now need channels the length of the canoe, which is much tougher to find. Many boater are nervous when they get turned around and feel that they should be facing forward to run a section. The canoe doesn't care which end is leading as it moves downstream so just look over your shoulder as you move in reverse. With poling we are able to take it one step farther, which is the ability to run upstream in reverse and believe it or not, it is a very useful and practical skill. Let's explore some of your options.

Running Sections in Reverse

There are many times when you will have to run a section backwards. In some cases it may be easier than running it forward because you have tremendous braking capacity for controlling speed. Keep yourself positioned as you would for forward climbing and just look over your shoulder. The pole should be positioned behind you in the same position as snubbing except you are facing upstream rather than downstream. The principle is the same in that you use short, quick snubs to control your descent. You have to be conscious of maintaining the same entry and exit angles of the pole to prevent it from pinning. If you feel you are descending too quickly, simply plant the pole and stop your progress. You can hold yourself stationary in moving water indefinitely as long as the canoe remains parallel to the main current. If you need to take a rest, ferry or side slip into the nearest eddy.

Make sure you have a stern heavy trim so the current will flow under the upstream end to prevent tracking. Watch for rocks just under the surface because, if hit, they can cause an immediate loss of balance, with you doing a seat plant on the bottom of the canoe or exiting out of the canoe.

Reverse Upstream in Reverse

There are many times when I have been picking my way down a complex rapid only to hit a dead end. Usually there is no room to eddy out or turn so I have to back out. If the current isn't too strong I can remain in my power poling stance and simply start backing up. I position the pole as if I was going to snub and apply reverse power plants instead to start climbing backwards. You can use the pole as a rudder by leaving it in the water after the power plant in front of you and move it left or right to correct your course. The difficulty with this is that because I have not changed my trim, the stern or upstream end wants to track because it is weighted. You can control it, but it is tough and requires constant attention to keep the bow under the stern. An easier move I use regularly is to do a "Rock Hop" over the center thwart, thus changing my trim immediately so the bow is now weighted. This is merely jumping over the center thwart so that you land in the same power position as previously except that you are facing the new stern. As you land, your feet should be against the chine of the canoe for stability and balance. You should still be one to two feet behind the thwart for proper trim. The original stern is no longer tracking and will swing around at will. Your body positioning is exactly like the normal power poling stance except you are facing backwards. Use the same principles for upstream climbs by crossing over from side to side to generate power while maintaining bow (or in this case, stern) control. Because you are close to the end of the canoe you have the ability to direct force on each plant by moving the top end of the pole left or right as you initiate the power plant. The pole will pass over the end of the canoe if you raise up on the pole enough. It is amazing how effective you are in this position and you can run up surprisingly difficult water and even climb drops like this. Don't forget to look over your shoulder to see where you are going.

Another alterntive, although you want to practice this in flat water first, is to perform a "rock-a-copter" to change ends and direction in the canoe at the same time. Once you realize that you have to back out, do a "Rock Hop" over the center thwart and while you are in the air, spin 180 degrees so that when you land, you will be perfectly positioned in the normal power poling stance and you can start climbing with the proper trim and body positioning. Use caution when first trying this but once you have it, you will find it the quickest and most efficient means of repositioning yourself at the other end of the canoe. And its a real crowd pleaser! But practice first!

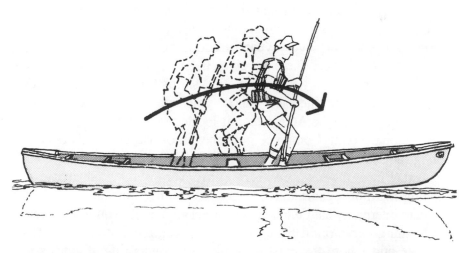

Figure 5-10 Rock Hop is used to quickly change trim positions from stern to bow if you have to suddenly revert to snubbing or to back upstream because of hitting a closed channel. Landing position should be the same as before jumping relative to correct power poling stance and distance from the center thwart.

6. INSTRUCTION AND RACING

There are two ways to best use this book. The first is to simply digest everything that you have read and get on the water to try it. Nothing beats just doing it, experimenting and learning through trial and error. As you try things, descriptions will begin to make more sense. You may need to constantly refer back to the text to clarify technique.

The second way is to join the American Canoe Association to have access to the list of instructional clinics that the National Poling Committee sponsors every year in cooperation with the National Instruction Committee. These are given in a number of locations across the country through a network of workshops hosted by committee members, private outfitters and canoe symposiums. A complete listing is available through the ACA which is located in Springfield , Virginia. The National Poling Commitee publishes information on a variety of poling subjects as well as additional instructional articles not covered in this text. I have always been a strong believer in taking advantage of existing learning opportunities rather than reinventing the wheel by trying to interpret what I think is the correct technique. You will shorten the learning curve dramatically by at least being exposed to what is possible and where the existing limits are concerning advances in technique.

Another altenative to helping shorten the learning curve as well as making practical use of this book is to get involved with the racing circuit throughout the east and the midwest sponsored by The American Canoe Association. Racing should not be looked at as threatening or as something that only the elite polers are involved in. Racing forces you to apply technique and form to practical use, all of which is described in this book. There is nothing written here that isn't used or hasn't been fine tuned through competition. By attending races you are exposed to some of the best canoe polers in the nation and a great deal of information and technique can be gleaned from them.

There are a number of different classes which take into consideration racing experience and ability level so that newcomers are competing against newcomers and not national champions. In all areas of a sport, recreational technique develops as a by product of racing because of the need for competitors to have an efficient and energy conserving style. They are concerned about covering the greatest amount of distance in as short a period of time while expending as little energy as possible. This can only be done through efficiency, which is learned through repeated practice sessions and muscle memory of technique that allows you to do a great deal of work with a limited output of energy and effort. The ultimate goal is to accomplish difficult moves while appearing as easy and effortless as possible, which is only possible through technique, finesse and style. Poling is nothing more than an application of angles and leverage. What makes some of us better than others is practice in all types of conditions, which racing provides. Racing will give you exposure to the fastest and easiest ways to run straight up or down river through wildwater classes, as well as developing the ability to dance a canoe through a complex rock garden with the exactness of ballerinas on stage (which is developed through slalom events). Nothing compares to the feeling of taking everything that the river can throw at you and exploiting a rock garden with spins, ferries, U turns, reverse moves, climbing drops frontwards and backwards, surfing holes and waves while doing rock hops and rock-a-copters in the middle of froth and foam.

So grab that big stick and remember to stand tall as you make the big push upriver. You will be greeted with a number of insightful remarks from floaters who are convinved you are moving in the wrong direction but pay them little heed. They are the ones moving in the wrong direction. The heritage of canoe sport started with the pole before the development of the paddle and continued with the exploration and mapping of the North American Continent through voyagers and explorers such as Lewis and Clark. It has been used commercially for moving freight up and down rivers as well as militarily in the Revolutionary War to transport troops and supplies. We are continuing with that tradition and heritage by being head and shoulders above all those paddlers as we climb drops and eddy hop against the relentless current.

INDEX